Smoothie Recipes

Easy Smoothie Recipes for Weight Loss, Better Skin and Feeling Great

Table of Contents

Introduction

I want to thank you for choosing this book, 'Smoothie Recipes - Easy Smoothie Recipes for Weight Loss, Better Skin and Feeling Great.'

Health is wealth and cannot be taken lightly. It is important, for everybody, to consume meals that can enhance overall well being and aid in the development of a lean and healthy body. One good way of doing so is through the consumption of smoothies. Smoothies are healthy drinks that can flush out toxins and keep the body in great shape.

Smoothies are easy to make and easier to consume. You don't have to spend a lot of time in the kitchen to prepare them and have them ready in a few minutes. They can be made using a variety of ingredients with three main components that are as follows.

Fruits/vegetables- You can choose any fruit or vegetable you like, and it is best to add 3 or 4 different varieties to make it a potent drink.

Yogurt - Yogurt is usually the base of the smoothie. It is best to pick Greek yogurt, as it is lighter than regular yogurt.

Protein powders- Protein powders can be added to smoothies to increase the fiber content and also boost up your protein intake.

Smoothies can be termed as elixirs because of the multiple health benefits they provide and should be made a part of every meal. Here are some of the benefits provided by smoothies.

Weight loss- Smoothies can provide a lasting solution to your weight loss issues. Smoothies contain a lot of fiber, which helps in loosening the fat and eliminating it from the body. You can make smoothies using fruits, vegetables, and powders and consume them on a daily basis to keep your digestive tract healthy.

Skin health-It is important to take good care of your skin right from a young age, as only then will you be able to prevent age related issues such as wrinkles, fine line, and spots. A good way of maintaining skin health is through the consumption of smoothies on a regular basis. Smoothies help in flushing out toxins and also promote healthy blood circulation. This helps in maintaining skin elasticity while reducing the occurrence of lines and wrinkles. Consuming smoothies made from fresh fruits can also prevent the onset of acne and help you maintain glowing, smooth skin.

Overall well being- Smoothies can help you fight away illnesses such as cancer and heart disease. This will enhance your longevity and help you lead a better life. You will also feel energetic and maintain good mental health. Your productivity will increase too!

As you can see, there are several benefits to consuming smoothies and without further ado, let us look at simple smoothies that you can put together.

Chapter 1: Easy Smoothie Recipes for Better Skin

Note: Always rinse the fruits and vegetables well before using. Peel the fruits and vegetables if desired.

Powerhouse Pumpkin Smoothie

Serves: 2

Ingredients:

- 1 cup canned pumpkin puree, frozen in ice cube tray
- 1 cup water
- 4 tablespoons ground flaxseeds
- 14 ounces 2% Greek yogurt
- ½ avocado, peeled, pitted, chopped
- 1 teaspoon pumpkin pie spice

Method:

1. Remove the frozen pumpkin puree cubes from the ice tray.
2. Add all the ingredients into a blender. Blend for 30-40 seconds or until smooth.
3. Add a little more water if you desire a smoothie of thinner consistency.
4. Pour into tall glasses and serve.

Berry Beauty Blast

Serves: 2

Ingredients:

- ½ cup blueberries, fresh or frozen
- ½ cup strawberries, fresh or frozen, sliced
- ½ cup raspberries, fresh or frozen
- 2 cups water
- ½ cup kale, discard hard stems and ribs, torn

Method:

1. Add all the ingredients into a blender. Blend for 30-40 seconds or until smooth.
2. Add a little more water if you desire a smoothie of thinner consistency.
3. Pour into tall glasses and serve with crushed ice.

Greens and Omega Skin Food Smoothie

Serves: 4

Ingredients:

- 1 avocado, peeled, pitted, chopped
- 4 leaves kale, discard hard ribs and stems
- 4 teaspoons flaxseed oil
- 3 cups coconut water or filtered water
- 2 tablespoons chia seeds
- 4 teaspoons chlorella powder
- 2 cups berries of your choice, fresh or frozen
- Ice cubes as required

Method:

1. Add all the ingredients into the blender and blend for 30-40 seconds or until smooth.
2. Add some more coconut water if your desire a smoothie of thinner consistency.
3. Pour into tall glasses and serve.

Mango Surprise Smoothie

Serves: 2

Ingredients:

- ½ cup ripe mango cubes
- 1 cup mango juice
- 2 tablespoons fresh lime juice
- ½ cup ripe avocado, peeled, pitted mashed
- ½ cup fat-free vanilla yogurt
- 2 tablespoons sugar
- 2 slices mango to garnish

Method:

1. Add all the ingredients into a blender. Blend for 30-40 seconds or until smooth.
2. Add a little more yogurt if you desire a smoothie of thinner consistency.
3. Pour into tall glasses. Garnish with mango slices and serve with crushed ice.

Green on Green on Green Smoothie

Serves: 1

Ingredients:

- 1 small cucumber, peeled, chopped
- ½ pear, cored, chopped
- 1 large leaf curly kale or lacianto kale, discard hard stem and rib, torn
- 2 ribs celery, chopped
- ¼ cup pineapple juice
- Juice of ½ lime
- Ice cubes as required

Method:

1. Add all the ingredients into a blender. Blend for 30-40 seconds or until smooth.
2. Add a little more pineapple juice if you desire a smoothie of thinner consistency.
3. Pour into a tall glass and serve.

Super Green Smoothie

Serves: 1

Ingredients:

- 2/3 cup kale leaves, discard hard stems and ribs
- 1 medium rib celery, chopped
- A handful flat leaf parsley
- 2/3 cup frozen mango pieces
- ½ cup fresh orange juice, chilled
- A handful mint leaves

Method:

1. Add all the ingredients into a blender. Blend for 30-40 seconds or until smooth.
2. Add a little more orange juice if you desire a smoothie of thinner consistency.
3. Pour into a tall glass and serve.

Happy Belly Smoothie

Serves: 2-3

Ingredients:

- 3 cups mango, peeled, pitted, cubed
- 2 cups frozen pineapple
- 2 cups fresh strawberries
- 2 cups kombucha brewed tea

Method:

1. Add all the ingredients into a blender. Blend for 30-40 seconds or until smooth.
2. Add a little more kombucha tea or water if you desire a smoothie of thinner consistency.
3. Pour into tall glasses and serve with crushed ice.

Gingered Cantaloupe Smoothie

Serves: 2

Ingredients:

- 1 cup cantaloupe, cubed
- 1 ½ tablespoons sugar
- 3 ounces low-fat plain yogurt
- ½ teaspoon fresh ginger, grated
- Ice cubes, as required

Method:

1. Add all the ingredients into a blender. Blend for 30-40 seconds or until smooth.
2. Add a little more yogurt if you desire a smoothie of thinner consistency.
3. Pour into tall glasses and serve.

Healthy High C Smoothie

Serves: 2

Ingredients:

- 2 cups kale, discard hard ribs and stems, torn
- 1 cup fresh orange juice
- 2 ribs celery, chopped
- 4 kiwifruits, peeled, chopped
- 1 cup fresh cilantro sprigs
- Ice cubes, as required

Method:

1. Add all the ingredients into a blender. Blend for 30-40 seconds or until smooth.
2. Add a little more orange juice if you desire a smoothie of thinner consistency.
3. Pour into tall glasses and serve.

Carrot Cake Smoothie

Serves: 2

Ingredients:

- 1 cup fresh carrot juice
- 4 tablespoons toasted wheat germ
- 2 tablespoons flaxseed oil
- 1 teaspoon glucomannan (optional)
- 2 scoops vanilla flavored whey protein powder
- 2 tablespoons soft cream cheese, regular fat
- ½ teaspoon ground cinnamon
- Ice cubes as required

Method:

1. Add all the ingredients into a blender. Blend for 30-40 seconds or until smooth.
2. Add a little more orange juice if you desire a smoothie of thinner consistency.
3. Pour into tall glasses and serve.

Winter Greens Smoothie

Serves: 1

Ingredients:

- ¼ cup fresh orange juice
- 2 tablespoons fresh carrot juice
- ½ cup kale, discard hard rib and stem, torn
- ½ cup fresh spinach, torn
- 2 small broccoli florets, sliced, frozen
- 1 small apple, cored, chopped
- 1 small banana, peeled, sliced, frozen

Method:

1. Add all the ingredients into a blender. Blend for 30-40 seconds or until smooth.
2. Add a little more orange juice if you desire a smoothie of thinner consistency.
3. Pour into a tall glass and serve with crushed ice.

Purple Smoothie

Serves: 2

Ingredients:

- 1 cup frozen blueberries
- 1 cup red cabbage, chopped
- 1 cup coconut water or almond milk

Method:

1. Add all the ingredients into a blender. Blend for 30-40 seconds or until smooth.
2. Pour into tall glasses and serve.

Skin Brightening Smoothie

Serves: 2

Ingredients:

- 2 teaspoons acai powder
- 2 teaspoons chia seeds
- 2 teaspoons raw cacao powder
- 2 teaspoons maca root powder
- ½ teaspoon ground cinnamon + extra to garnish
- 1 cup almond milk, unsweetened
- 1 cup coconut water
- 2 teaspoons goji berry
- 2 teaspoons ground flaxseed
- 2 teaspoons greens powder
- 4 walnuts, chopped
- Ice cubes, as required

Method:

1. Add all the ingredients into a blender. Blend for 30-40 seconds or until smooth.
2. Pour into tall glasses and serve garnished with ground cinnamon.

Smoothie for Acne Eczema and Anti-aging

Serves: 2

Ingredients:

- 1 large avocado, peeled, pitted, chopped
- 2 small cucumbers, scrubbed, chopped
- 4 kiwifruits, peeled, chopped
- 2 medium carrots, scrubbed, chopped
- 2 cups parsley leaves
- 2 tablespoons fresh ground flax seeds
- Almond milk/coconut water / plain yogurt/hemp milk, as required
- 2 teaspoons amla powder (Indian gooseberry powder)
- Stevia drops to taste
- 2 tablespoons extra virgin coconut oil

Method:

1. Choose the liquid of your choice and pour into the blender. Add rest the ingredients into the blender. Blend for 30-40 seconds or until smooth.
2. Pour into tall glasses and serve.

Clear Skin Smoothie

Serves: 2-3

Ingredients:

- 8 stalks celery, chopped
- 2 cups spinach, torn
- 2 apples, cored, chopped
- 2 leaves kale, discard hard stem and ribs, torn
- 2 bunches parsley, chopped
- 4 carrots, peeled, chopped
- 2 medium beets, peeled, chopped
- Juice of 2 lemons
- 1-inch piece ginger, peeled, sliced

Method:

1. Add all the ingredients into a blender. Blend for 30-40 seconds or until smooth.
2. Pour into tall glasses and serve with crushed ice.

Sweet potato and Carrot Smoothie for Stubborn Acne

Serves: 3

Ingredients:

- 2 large carrots, peeled, chopped
- 2 cups water
- 1 large sweet potato, scrubbed, grated
- 2 whole oranges, peeled, deseeded
- 2 teaspoons maple syrup or to taste
- 1 teaspoon ground cinnamon

Method:

1. Add all the ingredients into a blender. Blend for 30-40 seconds or until smooth.
2. Pour into tall glasses and serve with crushed ice.

Chapter 2: Smoothies for Weight Loss

Detox Probiotic Smoothie

Serves: 1

Ingredients:

- 1 cup unsweetened whole milk kefir, chilled
- A handful fresh cilantro or mint leaves
- 1 small cucumber, peel if desired, chopped
- Juice of a lemon
- A pinch salt
- ¼ teaspoon ground cumin
- A pinch cumin seeds to garnish (optional)
- Honey to taste (optional)

Method:

1. Add all the ingredients into a blender. Blend for 30-40 seconds or until smooth.
2. Pour into tall glasses and serve sprinkled with cumin seeds on top.

Kale and Sunflower Smoothie with Papaya and Pear

Serves: 2

Ingredients:

- 3 cups kale, discard hard stems and ribs, chopped
- 2 Bartlett pears, peeled, cored, chopped
- 1 cup ripe papaya, cubed or mango cubes
- 2 bananas, peeled, sliced, frozen
- 4 tablespoons sunflower seeds butter
- 2 cups coconut water
- 2 tablespoons honey or to taste

Method:

1. Steam the kale in your steaming equipment. Cool and add to a blender.
2. Add rest of the ingredients into the blender and blend for 30-40 seconds or until smooth.
3. Add some more milk if your desire a smoothie of thinner consistency.
4. Pour into tall glasses and serve with crushed ice.

Peaches and Cream Oatmeal Smoothie

Ingredients:

- 2 cups frozen peach slices
- 2 cups Greek yogurt
- ½ teaspoon vanilla
- ½ cup oatmeal
- 2 cups almond milk

Method:

1. Add all the ingredients into the blender and blend for 30-40 seconds or until smooth.
2. Add some more milk if your desire a smoothie of thinner consistency.
3. Pour into tall glasses and serve with crushed ice.

Vanilla Yogurt and Blueberry Smoothie

Serves: 2

Ingredients:

- 2 cups fresh blueberries
- 2 cups skim milk or soy milk
- 2 tablespoons flaxseed oil
- 12 ounces vanilla yogurt
- 1 tablespoon chia seeds or chia gel
- ½ teaspoon ground cinnamon
- Ice cubes, as required

Method:

1. Add all the ingredients except flaxseed oil into a blender and blend for 30-40 seconds or until smooth. Add a little more of the milk you are using if you desire a smoothie of thinner consistency.
2. Pour into tall glasses. Add flaxseed oil, stir and serve right away.

Watermelon Smoothie

Serves: 4

Ingredients:

- 8 cups watermelon, deseeded, chopped into small cubes
- 1/8 teaspoon black salt (optional)
- 1 ½ cups lemon sherbet or nonfat milk or low-fat vanilla yogurt

Method:

1. Add all the ingredients into a blender and blend for 30-40 seconds or until smooth.
2. Add more lemon sherbet if you desire a smoothie of thinner consistency.
3. Pour into tall glasses and serve with crushed ice.

Flat - Belly Smoothie

Serves: 3

Ingredients:

- 6 ounces vanilla flavored, nonfat Greek yogurt
- 1 cup frozen pineapple, chopped
- 1 cup frozen blueberries
- 2 cups kale, discard hard stems and ribs, torn
- 1 ½ cups water

Method:

1. Add all the ingredients into a blender and blend for 30-40 seconds or until smooth.
2. Add more water if you desire a smoothie of thinner consistency.
3. Pour into tall glasses and serve with crushed ice.

Blueberry Almond Butter Smoothie

Serves: 4

Ingredients:

- 2 bananas, peeled, chopped
- 6 dates, pitted, chopped
- 1 cup almond butter
- 2 cups blueberries
- 1 ½ cups almond milk
- 1 cup plain yogurt
- Ice cubes as required

Method:

1. Soak dates in a bowl of warm water for about 30 minutes to soften. Drain and add to a blender.
2. Add rest of the ingredients. Blend for 30-40 seconds or until smooth.
3. Add more almond milk if you desire a smoothie of thinner consistency.
4. Pour into tall glasses and serve.

Peachy Keen Breakfast Smoothie

Serves: 2

Ingredients:

- 4 medium ripe peach, pitted, chopped
- 12 almonds, chopped
- Soy milk, as required
- 2 tablespoons flax seeds
- 3 cups vanilla flavored Greek yogurt

Method:

1. Pour enough soy milk as desired into the blender. Add rest of the ingredients into the blender and blend for 30-40 seconds or until smooth.
2. Pour into tall glasses and serve with crushed ice.

Peanut Butter and Jelly Protein Smoothie

Serves: 2

Ingredients:

- 2 cups frozen berries of your choice
- 2 scoops vanilla flavored whey protein powder
- 2 cups soy milk
- 2 tablespoons unsalted, natural peanut butter
- 4 tablespoons rolled oats

Method:

1. Add all the ingredients into a blender and blend for 30-40 seconds or until smooth.
2. Add more soy milk if you desire a smoothie of thinner consistency.
3. Pour into tall glasses and serve with crushed ice.

Blueberry Tofu High Protein Smoothie

Serves: 2

Ingredients:

- 1 1/3 cups blueberries
- 2 tablespoons honey
- 1 large banana, peeled, sliced
- Soy milk, as required
- 12 ounces soft silken tofu

Method:

1. Pour enough soy milk as desired into the blender. Add rest of the ingredients into the blender and blend for 30-40 seconds or until smooth.
2. Pour into tall glasses and serve with crushed ice.

Hydrating Summer Blast

Serves: 2

Ingredients:

- 1 cup ripe papaya cubes
- 1 large apple, cored, chopped
- 8 large strawberries, hulled, chopped
- 2 kiwifruits, peeled, chopped
- Juice of a lemon
- 1 ½ cups coconut water or water
- ½ teaspoon sea salt
- A pinch of pepper powder

Method:

1. Add all the ingredients into the blender and blend for 30-40 seconds or until smooth.
2. Add some more coconut water if your desire a smoothie of thinner consistency
3. Pour into tall glasses and serve with crushed ice.

Banana, Carrot – Orange and Seeds Smoothie

Serves: 2

Ingredients:

- 2 bananas, peeled, sliced
- 1 orange, peeled, deseeded, chopped
- 4 cups spinach, washed
- 4-5 small carrots, scrubbed, chopped
- 1 teaspoon pumpkin seeds
- 1 teaspoon hemp seeds
- 2 teaspoons flax seeds
- 1 cup Greek yogurt
- Low-fat milk, as required

Method:

1. Pour enough milk as desired into the blender. Add rest of the ingredients into the blender and blend for 30-40 seconds or until smooth.
2. Pour into tall glasses and serve with crushed ice.

Kale and Apple Green Detox Smoothie

Serves: 2

Ingredients:

- 1 1/3 cups almond milk, unsweetened
- 3 cups kale, discard hard ribs and stems, chopped or torn
- 1 red or green apple, cored, chopped
- 2 stalks celery, chopped
- 2 teaspoons honey (optional)
- 2 tablespoons ground flax seeds
- Ice cubes as required

Method:

1. Add all the ingredients into the blender and blend for 30-40 seconds or until smooth.
2. Add some more almond milk if your desire a smoothie of thinner consistency
3. Pour into tall glasses and serve with crushed ice.

Fat burning Green Tea and Vegetable Smoothie

Serves: 2

Ingredients:

- 4 cups cauliflower florets
- 6 cups broccoli florets
- 2 cups pineapple pieces
- Freshly brewed caffeinated green tea, as required
- 2 pineapple spears
- Ice cubes, as required

Method:

1. Pour enough green tea into the blender. Add cauliflower, broccoli and pineapple pieces into the blender and blend for 30-40 seconds or until smooth.
2. Pour into tall glasses. Place the pineapple spears on the rim of the glass.
3. Serve.

Green Protein Detox Smoothie

Serves: 2

Ingredients:

- 1 cup almond milk, unsweetened
- 2 bananas, peeled, sliced
- 1 cup kale, discard hard ribs and stems, chopped
- 1 cup chard, discard hard ribs and stems, chopped
- 2 cups spinach, chopped

Method:

1. Add all the ingredients into the blender and blend for 30-40 seconds or until smooth.
2. Add some more almond milk if your desire a smoothie of thinner consistency
3. Pour into tall glasses and serve with crushed ice.

Peanut Butter and Banana Smoothie

Serves: 2

Ingredients:

- 1 cup fat-free milk
- 4 tablespoons creamy, natural peanut butter, unsalted
- 1 cup fat-free plain yogurt
- ½ very ripe banana, peeled, chopped
- 2 tablespoons honey
- Ice cubes

Method:

1. Add all the ingredients into the blender and blend for 30-40 seconds or until smooth.
2. Add some more milk if your desire a smoothie of thinner consistency.
3. Pour into tall glasses and serve with crushed ice.

Chapter 3: Smoothies for Feeling Great

Tropical Spinach Smoothie

Serves: 1

Ingredients:

- 2 cups baby spinach
- 1 small banana, peeled, sliced
- ¼ cup plain Greek yogurt
- ½ cup water
- Ice cubes as required
- 10 ounces pineapple juice

Method:

1. Add all the ingredients into the blender and blend for 30-40 seconds or unti smooth.
2. Add more juice if you like a smoothie of thinner consistency.
3. Pour into tall glasses and serve with crushed ice.

Green Smoothie

Serves: 1

Ingredients:

- 1 ripe banana, peeled, sliced
- 3 strawberries, hulled, chopped
- 1 medium peach, pitted, chopped
- ½ cup water
- A handful spinach or any other greens of your choice

Method:

1. Add all the ingredients into the blender and blend for 30-40 seconds or until smooth.
2. Add some more milk if your desire a smoothie of thinner consistency.
3. Pour into a tall glass and serve with crushed ice.

Hi there! Are you enjoying this book? Are you receiving benefit? Please leave a review in Amazon if you are by clicking here..

Sunrise Smoothie Parfait

Serves: 2

Ingredients:

- 1 cup frozen blueberries, unsweetened
- 1 cup ripe mango, peeled, pitted, chopped
- 1 cup frozen pineapple cubes
- 4 tablespoons frozen acai pulp
- ¼ cup cold water
- 1 tablespoon light agave nectar
- 2 tablespoons fresh lime juice
- ½ cup coconut water
- 2 tablespoons toasted wheat germ
- 4 tablespoons flaked coconut, unsweetened
- Ice cubes as required

Method:

1. Place 2 glasses in the refrigerator to chill.
2. Add blueberries, acai pulp, and agave nectar and cold water into a blender and blend for 30-40 seconds or until smooth.
3. Pour into the chilled glasses.
4. Now clean the blender. Rinse well.
5. Add mango, wheat germ, lime juice and ice into the blender. Blend for 30-40 seconds or until smooth.
6. Divide and pour over the blueberry layer. Do not stir.
7. Now clean the blender again. Rinse well.
8. Add pineapple cubes, coconut water, and flaked coconut into the blender. Blend for 30-40 seconds or until smooth.
9. Divide and pour over the mango layer. Do not stir.
10. Serve immediately.

Tropical Treat Smoothie

Serves: 2

Ingredients:

- 2 cups fresh pineapple cubes
- 2 pineapple wedges to garnish
- 1 cup coconut sorbet
- A handful mint leaves
- 1 cup soft silken tofu
- ¼ cup cold water
- 2 tablespoons fresh lime juice
- 1 teaspoon fresh ginger, minced

Method:

1. Add all the ingredients into the blender and blend for 30-40 seconds or until smooth.
2. Pour into tall glasses and serve with crushed ice.

Ultra Chocolate Smoothie

Serves: 2

Ingredients:

- 1 ½ cups chocolate flavored low-fat frozen yogurt
- 1 cup almond milk, unsweetened
- 4 tablespoons cocoa, unsweetened
- Dark chocolate shavings to garnish

Method:

1. Place 2 glasses in the refrigerator to chill.
2. Add frozen yogurt, milk, and cocoa into a blender. Blend for 30-40 seconds or until smooth.
3. Pour into the chilled glasses. Garnish with chocolate shavings and serve.

Double C Smoothie

Serves: 2

Ingredients:

- 2 cups ripe papaya (preferably the strawberry variety), peeled, chopped
- 2 kiwifruits
- 3 tablespoons light agave nectar, divided
- ½ cup vanilla flavored low-fat frozen yogurt of kefir
- 2 tablespoons lime fruit

Method:

1. Place 2 glasses in the refrigerator in the refrigerator to chill.
2. Peel the kiwi fruits. Cut 2-4 thin round slices of the kiwi and set aside to garnish. Chop the remaining kiwi.
3. Add papaya, frozen yogurt, 2 tablespoons agave nectar and lime juice into the blender. Blend for 30-40 seconds or until smooth.
4. Divide and pour into the chilled glasses.
5. Now clean and rinse the blender.
6. Add kiwifruits and 1 tablespoon agave nectar into the blender. Blend for 30-40 seconds or until smooth.
7. Divide and pour over the papaya layer in the glasses. Do not stir.
8. Garnish with kiwi slices and serve immediately.

Berry Power-Up Smoothie

Serves: 2

Ingredients:

- ½ cup frozen strawberries, unsweetened
- ½ cup frozen raspberries, unsweetened
- ½ cup frozen blueberries, unsweetened
- ½ cup pomegranate juice
- 2 tablespoons honey
- 2 tablespoons vanilla flavored whey protein powder
- 2 tablespoons fresh lemon juice

Method:

1. Add all the ingredients into the blender and blend for 30-40 seconds or until smooth.
2. Pour into tall glasses and serve with crushed ice.

Spring Salad Smoothie

Serves: 2

Ingredients:

- 1 cup fresh carrot juice
- ½ cup baby spinach or Mache (corn lettuce)
- 6 tablespoons frozen wheatgrass juice, thawed
- 3 tablespoons fresh lemon juice
- 1 teaspoon matcha tea powder
- ¼ cup fresh cilantro
- 1 small ripe avocado, peeled, pitted, chopped
- 2 tablespoons ground flaxseeds
- A pinch fine sea salt
- Ice cube as required

Method:

1. Add all the ingredients into the blender and blend for 30-40 seconds or until smooth.
2. Pour into tall glasses and serve with crushed ice.

Matcha Green Tea Frappe

Serves: 4

Ingredients:

- 1 cup raw almonds, soaked in water for 7-8 hours
- 4-6 teaspoons matcha green tea powder
- 4 cups coconut water
- 2 tablespoons agave nectar or coconut sugar maple syrup
- 2 teaspoons vanilla extract
- 2 packets stevia powder (optional)
- A large pinch salt
- Ice cubes as required

Method:

1. Drain and rinse the almonds. Transfer to the blender.
2. Add coconut water. Blend for 30-40 seconds or until smooth.
3. Pass the blended mixture nut milk bag or line a strainer with cheesecloth and then strain. Squeeze the nut milk bag to remove as much liquid as possible.
4. Clean and rinse the blender.
5. Add the strained almond milk into the blender. Add rest of the ingredients into the blender. Blend for 30-40 seconds or until smooth.
6. Pour into tall glasses and serve.

Electrolyte Green Goddess Blender Tonic

Serves: 4

Ingredients:

- 2 lemons, peeled, quartered, deseeded
- 2 stalks celery, chopped
- 1 pear, cored, chopped
- 6 romaine lettuce leaves, shredded
- 1 cup parsley, chopped
- 1 cucumber, chopped
- A large pinch sea salt.

Method:

1. Add all the ingredients into the blender and blend for 30-40 seconds or until smooth.
2. Pour into tall glasses and serve with crushed ice.

Peach Rooibos Probiotic Smoothie

Serves: 4

Ingredients:

- 4 rooibos tea bags
- 2 bananas, peeled, sliced, frozen
- 4 cups peaches, pitted, chopped, fresh or frozen
- 4 capsules probiotics
- 4 cups hot water

Method:

1. Place the tea bags in hot water for 5 minutes. Discard the tea bags. Add some ice cubes into the freshly made tea.
2. When the tea is cold, transfer to a blender. Add rest of the ingredients. Blend for 30-40 seconds or until smooth.
3. Add more water if you want a smoothie of thinner consistency.
4. Pour into tall glasses and serve.

Kombucha Mega C Smoothie

Serves: 4

Ingredients:

- 7 ounces frozen acai berry puree
- ½ cup parsley, chopped
- 2 bananas, peeled, sliced
- 2 cups strawberries, hulled, chopped, fresh or frozen
- ½ cup almonds, chopped
- 2 bottles (16 ounces each) kombucha tea

Method:

1. Add all the ingredients into the blender and blend for 30-40 seconds or until smooth.
2. Pour into tall glasses and serve with crushed ice.

Summer in a Cup Smoothie

Serves: 4

Ingredients:

- 2 large ripe bananas, peeled, sliced, frozen
- 2 ½ cups frozen raspberries
- 1 ½ cups orange juice
- 1 cup pomegranate juice
- 1 ½ cups almond milk, unsweetened

Method:

1. Add all the ingredients into the blender and blend for 30-40 seconds or until smooth.
2. Add more milk or any of the 2 juices if you like a smoothie of thinner consistency
3. Pour into tall glasses and serve with crushed ice.

Strawberry Banana Mango Lava Smoothie

Serves: 3-4

Ingredients:

- 10 large strawberries, hulled, chopped
- 3 bananas, peeled, sliced, frozen
- 1 champagne mango, peeled, pitted, chopped
- 1 cup Greek yogurt
- 1 cup light coconut milk
- 1 teaspoon vanilla extract
- Ice cubes as required

Method:

1. Place 3-4 glasses in the refrigerator to chill.
2. Add strawberries into a blender and blend for 30-40 seconds or until smooth.
3. Divide and pour into the chilled glasses.
4. Now clean the blender. Rinse well.
5. Add mango, yogurt, coconut milk, vanilla and ice into the blender. Blend for 30-40 seconds or until smooth.
6. Divide and pour over the strawberry layer. Do not stir.
7. Serve immediately.

Raw Banana Bread Shakes

Serves: 4-6

Ingredients:

For Walnut milk:

- 6 cups water
- 2 cups walnuts, soaked in water for 4-5 hours

For raw banana bread shake:

- 4 cups bananas, peeled, sliced, fresh or frozen
- A pinch fresh nutmeg, grated
- 2 tablespoons maple syrup (optional)
- 4 cacao nibs + extra to garnish
- 2 teaspoons ground cinnamon
- 1 teaspoon vanilla powder or vanilla extract
- Ice cubes as required

Method:

1. Strain the walnuts and transfer to a blender. Add water. Blend for 30-40 seconds or until smooth.
2. Pass the blended mixture nut milk bag or line a strainer with cheesecloth and then strain. Squeeze the nut milk bag to remove as much liquid as possible.
3. Clean and rinse the blender.
4. Add the strained walnut milk into the blender. Add rest of the ingredients except cacao nibs into the blender. Blend for 30-40 seconds or until smooth.
5. Add cacao nibs and pulse for a few seconds. The cacao nibs should only be broken into smaller pieces.
6. Pour into tall glasses and serve garnished with cacao nibs.

Peach Melba Sunrise Smoothie

Serves: 4

Ingredients:

- 1 ½ cups frozen raspberries
- 2 peaches, peeled, pitted, chopped
- 2 cups almond milk
- 2 tablespoons lemon juice
- 2 cups orange juice
- 2 teaspoons vanilla extract
- 2 tablespoons maple syrup
- Ice cubes as required

Method:

1. Place 4 glasses in the refrigerator to chill.
2. Add raspberries, almond milk, lemon juice and vanilla extract into a blender and blend for 30-40 seconds or until smooth.
3. Divide and pour into the chilled glasses.
4. Now clean the blender. Rinse well.
5. Add peach, orange juice, and ice into the blender. Blend for 30-40 seconds or until smooth.
6. Divide and pour over the raspberry layer. Swirl lightly.
   Serve immediately.

Conclusion

The primary objective of this book was to leave you with simple smoothie recipes that you can prepare and consume on a daily basis. Do not limit yourself to just these recipes and come up with some of your own. As long as you keep the ingredients fresh and healthy, you can make as many different varieties of smoothies as you like.

You can ask your family members to help you out and together; you can make and enjoy the smoothies. Some of these smoothies can be treated as whole meals and replace your breakfast or dinner.

You will begin to notice the benefits of taking up the smoothie diet in no time and will motivate you to stick with it for life. Hope you have a fun time making the smoothies and recling in good health.

Finally, if you enjoyed this book, then I'd like to ask you for a favor, would you be kind enough to leave a review for this book on Amazon? It'd be greatly appreciated!

Thank you and happy smoothie days!

Made in the USA
Middletown, DE
27 July 2018